A SIMPLE GUIDE TO BIBLICAL ISRAEL

What You Need to Know Before You Go

G. Michael Cocoris

© 2026 euros by G. Michael Cocoris

All rights reserved. This publication may not be reproduced (in whole or in part, edited, or revised) in any way, form, or means, including, but not limited to electronic, mechanical, photocopying, recording or any kind of storage and retrieval system *for sale*, except for brief quotations in printed reviews, without the written permission of G. Michael Cocoris, 2016 Euclid #20, Santa Monica, CA 90405, michaelcocoris@gmail.com, or his appointed representatives. Permission is hereby granted, however, for the reproduction of the whole or parts of the whole without changing the content in any way for *free distribution,* provided all copies contain this copyright notice in its entirety. Permission is also granted to charge for the cost of copying.

Unless otherwise indicated, all Scripture quotations are taken from the New King James Version ®, Copyright © 1979, 1980, 1982 by Thomas Nelson, Inc. Used by permission. All rights reserved.

Cover and interior design by John T. Cocoris

Printed in the United States

TABLE OF CONTENTS

Chapter 1	Introduction	1
Chapter 2	The History of The Land	5
Chapter 3	A Historical Outline of The Bible	13
Chapter 4	The Trials of Christ	15
Chapter 5	The Stations of The Cross	17
Chapter 6	Major Biblical Sites	19
Chapter 7	The Spiritual Benefit	31
About The Author		35

Chapter 1

Introduction

Taking a tour of Israel is educational, inspiring—and can be confusing. Several issues cause the confusion.

The Problem

Professional guides cover a massive amount of information. Most Christian tourists from America are overwhelmed. It has been described as drinking from a fire hydrant.

For example, the history of the land extends from the time of Abraham to the present, a period of 4000 years. So, on the tour, the guide may point out something that pertains to the Crusader period one minute and something that pertains to the Turkish period the next.

For another thing, there are multiple biblical events at some sites. For example, when standing on the Mount of Olives looking at the Temple site, which now contains the Dome of the Rock, you are looking at Mount Moriah, where Abraham went to offer Isaac (Gen. 22). It is also the same site where David built an altar (2 Sam. 24:21). Later, Solomon built the Temple there (1 Chron. 21:28). That Temple was destroyed in 586 BC. Later, it was rebuilt and destroyed again in AD 70. The Dome of the Rock was built in AD 691.

Another example is the shepherd's field in Bethlehem. It's the same field where Ruth met Boaz, David shepherded sheep, and the angels told the shepherds about the birth of Christ.

To complicate matters, no tour can be in chronological order. The tour may be organized so that tourists visit Nazareth, where Jesus grew up, and Capernaum, where Jesus lived, before visiting Bethlehem, where Jesus was born.

The Solution

At least part of the solution is to know before you go, the history of the land and the history during biblical times. In chapter 1, a brief history of the land is laid out, and in chapter 2, an outline of biblical history is given.

It is also helpful to know about the six trials of Christ. Tours do not cover all six sites, but they do include the house of Caiaphas, where one of the six trials occurred.

In addition, knowing about The Way of Sorrows, also known as the Via Dolorosa, before you go will help you understand what is going on as you retrace the steps of Jesus from His condemnation to His body being placed in the tomb.

Many books have been written as guides to touring Israel. The advantage of those books over this one is that they include pictures. Consulting them is a good idea because of the pictures. What this book does that others do not is provide a simple outline of the land's history and a brief historical outline of the biblical events. It will also give you a brief description of the major biblical sites,

Introduction

more than you will cover on your tour, but it is not exhaustive.

A Suggestion

Here is a step-by-step guide to preparing for a tour of Israel.

1. From the brochure of the tour you're about to take in Israel, list all of the various **places** you will see.
2. Determine the biblical **events** that took place in each of those places (see chapter 5 below)
3. Place each of those events within the **historical period** (see chapter 2 below).
4. From other books, Google, or YouTube, view **pictures** of sites. For example, see photos of the synagogue at Capernaum.
5. Read the **Scripture** about those events.

The more you know before you go, the more you will get out of the tour.

Chapter 2

The History of The Land

The city of Pensacola Florida, the city in which I was born and reared, is called the City of Five Flags, because five nations ruled over it: Spain (1559-1719, 1722-1763, and 1781-1821), France (1719-1722), Britain (1763-1781), United States (1821-1861), the Confederate States of America (1861-1865), and the United States (1865 to present).

Likewise, the "Holy Land" has been occupied by various inhabitants and ruled over by multiple nations. It has been known as Canaan, the Land of Israel, the Holy Land, and Palestine. Here is a list of the major groups that have occupied or controlled the land.

Canaanites

From a biblical point of view, the history of the land begins with God telling Abram to leave his own country and go "to a land that I will show you" (Gen. 12:1). At that time, the Canaanites, a diverse group of Semitic-speaking peoples, occupied the land. They were not unified as a single nation. They occupied the land as rival, fortified city-states, such as Jericho, Hazor, Megiddo, and Gezer.

Abram moved to Canaan, but God did not give him or his immediate descendants the land of Canaan. Rather, He said, "Know certainly that your descendants will be strangers in a land that is not theirs and will serve them and they will afflict them four hundred years, and also the nation whom they serve I will judge; afterward they shall come out with great possessions" (Gen. 15:13-14). This prophecy was fulfilled when the children of Israel were in Egypt (the Hebrew word rendered "afflicted" in Gen. 15:13 is used in Ex. 1:11 to describe the experience of the Israelites in Egypt). The four hundred years is a round number for four hundred and thirty years (Ex. 12:40; Gal. 3:17). In 1447 BC, God did indeed judge the Egyptians (Ex. 7:1-12:34), and the Israelites did depart with great possessions (Ex. 12:35-36).

Israelites (1407 to 722/605 BC)

From 1407 to 1400 BC, under Joshua's leadership, the Israelites conquered the land of Canaan. They occupied the entire land until 722 BC. During this period, the Israelites were ruled by judges and then kings, including Saul, David, and Solomon.

When Solomon died, the nation was divided into the Northern and Southern Kingdoms (931 BC). In 722 BC, the Assyrians conquered the Northern Kingdom, but the Southern Kingdom was not conquered until 605 BC

Assyrians (722 to 605 BC)

After the Assyrians conquered the Northern Kingdom, they attempted to conquer the Southern Kingdom, but God supernaturally defeated them. So, from 722 to 605 BC, the Assyrians ruled the Northern Kingdom, while the Israelites remained in the Southern Kingdom.

Babylonians (605 to 539 BC)

The Babylonians conquered the Assyrians and then attacked the Southern Kingdom of Israel in 605, 598, and 586 BC. Many of the Israelites were taken into exile in Babylon, and in 586 BC, the Temple was destroyed.

Persians (539 to 332 BC)

The Persians conquered the Babylonians and allowed the Israelites to return and rebuild the Temple, but the land remained under Persian control.

Greeks (332 to 167 BC)

Alexander the Great conquered Persia in 332 BC. The Hellenistic control of the land was later split between Ptolemaic and Seleucid rule.

Israelites (167 to 63 BC)

For a brief period between 167 and 63 BC, the Israelites enjoyed independence.

Romans (63 BC to AD 476)

In 63 BC, the Romans conquered the land and established Judea as a province. The land was under Roman rule during the lifetime of Jesus Christ and during the period covered by the book of Acts. After putting down a Jewish revolt in 135 BC, Hadrian named the land Palestine.

Byzantine Empire (476 to 1453)

The city of Rome fell in AD 476. The eastern part of the Roman Empire, however, survived. Its capital was Constantinople. The people used the term "Roman Empire" and called themselves Romans. The term "Byzantine Empire" was not coined until after the Ottoman Empire conquered Constantinople in 1453. Although the Byzantine Empire existed for about a thousand years during the Middle Ages, it was not always unified, nor did it always control the land of Israel.

Muslim Rule (634-1099)

After the death of Muhammad in 632, the Muslim leadership

passed to Caliph Abu Bakr. Once Abu Bakr's sovereignty over Arabia was secured, he initiated a war in the east, invading Iraq and the Byzantine Empire. The Muslims conquered and controlled Jerusalem in 638.

Crusaders (1099-1291)

Throughout Europe, there arose a cry to free the Holy Land from Islamic control. The result was the crusades that lasted from 1095 to 1291. There were many expeditions called "crusades," but there were seven major crusades. In the spring of 1097, the first organized group of crusaders arrived at Constantinople. It consisted of 275,000 of the best warriors from every land in Europe. They took Nicaea, Antioch (1098), and Jerusalem (1099). The kingdom of Jerusalem lasted until 1187. In 1187, the Muslim leader Saladin recaptured Jerusalem. The kingdom of Jerusalem came to an end, but there were other crusades. The Crusades lasted for two centuries and cost Europe nearly five million lives.

Restored Muslim Control (1291-1517)

The Crusades failed to free the Holy Land from Muslim rule. In 1291, the Crusade era came to an end with the fall of Acre to the Muslims under Saladin and later under Mamluk military rule.

Ottoman Empire (1517-1917)

The Ottoman Empire, also known as the Turkish Empire, was founded by Osman, a tribal leader. The Ottomans ended the Byzantine Empire with the conquest of Constantinople by Mehmed II in 1453. The Ottoman Empire ruled the land from 1517 to 1917.

Between 1870 and 1897, 20 Jewish towns were established in the land. In 1897, Theodor Herzl founded the World Zionist Organization, whose objective was to create a Jewish state with as much land, as many Jews, and as fewArabs as possible. The Zionist claim to the land was based on the premise that the Jewish right to the land outweighed that of the Arabs.

British Mandate (1917-1948)

In November 1914, Britain declared war on the Ottoman Empire. Immediately after that, the British war cabinet began to consider the future of the land, which at the time had a small minority of Jews. In 1917, the Ottoman Empire, which had ruled the land for four centuries, was defeated.

In November 1917, Arthur Balfour, the British foreign secretary, wrote a letter to Lord Rothschild, a leader of the British Jewish community. In it, the British government announced its support for the establishment of a "national home for the Jewish people." This became known as the Balfour Declaration.

In April 1920, the League of Nations issued The Mandate for Palestine, which assigned to Britain the administration of the territories of Palestine and Transjordan. Britain's civil administration began in Palestine in July 1920 and in Transjordan in April 1921. The mandate was in force for Palestine from September 29, 1923, to May 15, 1948, and for Transjordan until May 25, 1946. The objective of the mandates was to provide "administrative advice and assistance by a Mandatory until such time as they are able to stand alone." It also required Britain to put into effect the Balfour Declaration's "national home for the Jewish people."

In November 1947, the United Nations passed the Partition Plan for Palestine, which envisaged the creation of separate Jewish and Arab states with Jerusalem transferred to UN trusteeship. Two weeks later, Britain announced that the British Mandate would end on May 15, 1948.

State of Israel

In 1948, on the last day of the British Mandate, the State of Israel declared its independence and the civil war in Mandatory Palestine became an international conflict. During the war, Israel expanded its territory to control over 78% of former Mandatory Palestine. As a result of the 1948 war, only an estimated 160,000 of 870,000 Arabs in the territory remained, forming an Arab minority in Israel. Thus, on May 15, 1948, Israel became a state. It is the only instance in history of a small nation being scattered and succeeding in reestablishing itself as a nation.

From 1948 to 1967, control of the land was divided between Israel, Jordan (the West Bank), and Egypt (Gaza). As a result of the Six-Day War in 1967, Israel occupied the West Bank, East Jerusalem, and the Gaza Strip.

Summary: From the time of Abraham to the present, the land has been occupied and controlled by many nations, including Jews, Christians, and later, Muslim Arabs.

Chapter 3

A Historical Outline of The Bible

The major places visited on tours of Israel are listed here by their historical period.

I. **The Patriarchs** (Genesis 12-50)   2167-1806 BC
Abraham was to sacrifice Isaac on
Mount Moriah (Genesis 22)

II. **The Exodus** (Exodus-Deuteronomy)   1527-1407 BC

III. **The Conquest** (Joshua)   1407-1400 BC
Jericho (Joshua 2)

IV. **The Judges** (Judges)   1375-1043 BC
Gideon's Spring (Judges 7)
Boaz's field (Ruth)

V. **The United Kingdom** (1 Samuel-1 Kings 11)   1043-931 BC
David at Ein Gedi (1 Samuel 24; Psalm 57. 142)
Solomon's Megiddo (1 Kings 4:12, 9:15)

VI. **The Divided Kingdom** (1 Kings 12-2 Kings 16)   931-605 BC
Ahab's water tunnel (1 Kings 22:39)
Hezekiah's wall (2 Chronicles 32:5; Isaiah 22 10)

VII. **The Captivity** (2 Kings 17- 25)   605-536 BC

VIII. **The Restoration** (Ezra-Nehemiah)   536-400 BC

IX. **The Ministry of Christ** (Matthew-John)   6/5 BC-AD 30/33

1. Bethlehem (Matthew 2:1-6; Luke 2:4-7)
2. Nazareth (Matthew 2:23; Luke 2:39: 4:16)
3. Cana (John 2:1, 4:46)
4. Capernaum (Matthew 4:13; Mark 1:21)
5. Caesarea Philippi (Matthew 16:13)
6. Upper Room (John 13-14) (then John 15)
7. Mount of Olives (Matthew 24-25)
8. Garden of Gethsemane (John 17)
9. Caiaphas's house (Matthew 26:57)
10. Stations of the Cross (Matthew 27; Mark 15; Luke 23; and John 19)
11. Calvary (Matthew 27:33; Mark 15:22; Luke 23:33; John 19:17)
12. Tomb (Matthew 27:57-60; Mark 15:46; Luke 23:50-53; John 19:38-42).

X. The Acts of the Apostles (Acts)　　　　AD30/33-60
　　Caesarea (Acts 8:40: 10:24; 23:23)

Chapter 4

The Trials Of Christ

Jesus was arrested in the Garden of Gethsemane. Then, over the next 8 to 12 hours, He appeared in six trials: three Jewish (religious) hearings and three Roman (civil) proceedings. The religious trials sought a blasphemy conviction, while the Roman trials focused on sedition charges.

Jewish Trials

1. Before Annas (Jn. 18:12-14) This was an initial, informal examination before the former High Priest. Decision: execute Jesus.

2. Before Caiaphas (Mt. 26:57-68) This was a nighttime hearing where witnesses were sought and Jesus was questioned about His identity. Decision: Death Sentence for the charge of blasphemy, because Jesus proclaimed Himself the Messiah, God the Son. Tours visit the house of Caiaphas and the prison where it is assumed that Jesus spent the night after the trial.

3. Before the Sanhedrin (Mt. 27:1-2; Lk. 22:63-71) This was a formal, early morning gathering to ratify the earlier verdict of blasphemy. Decision: death.

Roman Trials

4. Before Pilate (Jn. 18:28-38) The Roman governor initially found no guilt in Jesus regarding charges of treason. Decision: not guilty.

5. Before Herod Antipas (Lk. 23:6-12) Pilate sent Jesus to Herod, who questioned Him, mocked Him, and sent Him back. Decision: not guilty

6. Before Pilate (Jn. 18:39-19:6) Decision: not guilty. Under pressure from the crowd, Pilate handed Him over to be crucified (Mt. 27:26).

Summary: The six trials violated both Jewish and Roman legal procedures, lacking proper defense, witnesses for the accused, and, in some cases, proper timing.

Chapter 5

The Stations of The Cross

The Stations of the Cross, also known as the Via Dolorosa, are a series of events from Jesus' condemnation to His burial. Early Christians visited these sites. Francis of Assisi popularized visiting the sites with devotion. There are several versions of the Stations of the Cross. In 1731, Pope Clement XII established the number at 14. In the traditional form, stations 3, 4, 6, 7, and 9 are not explicitly biblical (the ones underlined). The traditional form of the Stations of the Cross is as follows:

1. The Antonia Fortress, where Pilate condemned Jesus.
   The Umariya Muslim Elementary School.
2. Lithostrotos, where Jesus takes up the cross.
   The Church of the Condemnation and Flagellation. Lithostrotos is the paved courtyard of the Antonia fortress. "Ecce Homo" means "behold the man." The Ecce Homo Arch is traditionally where Pontius Pilate presented Jesus to the crowd. The arch was constructed as part of a three-arched victory gate built by Hadrian in AD 135.
3. <u>Jesus falls for the first time.</u>
   The Polish Biblical Chapel at the corner of El-Wad St.

4. <u>Jesus meets His mother, Mary.</u>
   The Armenian Catholic Church of Our Lady of the Spasm.
5. Simon of Cyrene is forced to carry the cross.
   The Corner of Via Dolorosa and El-Wad St.
6. <u>Veronica wipes blood off Jesus' face.</u>
   The Chapel of the Holy Face on Via Dolorosa St.
7. <u>Jesus falls for the second time.</u>
   The Intersection of Via Dolorosa and Khan es-Zeit St.
8. Jesus spoke to the women of Jerusalem.
   The Greek Orthodox Monastery of Saint Charalambos.
9. <u>Jesus falls for the third time.</u>
   The entrance to the Coptic Patriarchate (near the Holy Sepulchre roof).
10. Jesus is stripped of His garments.
    The Chapel of the Franks (outside the Holy Sepulchre entrance).
11. Calvary. Jesus is nailed to the cross.
    The altar inside the Church of the Holy Sepulchre.
12. Calvary. Jesus dies on the cross.
    The Greek Orthodox Calvary Altar (above the rock of Golgotha).
13. Calvary. Jesus' body is removed from the cross.
    The Stone of Anointing (or the Shrine of Our Lady of Sorrows).
14. Holy supplicant. Jesus' body is placed in the tomb. of Joseph of Arimathea. The tomb in the church rotunda.

Chapter 6

Major Biblical Sites

A short tour of 10 days or 2 weeks cannot possibly cover all the biblical sites in Israel. Here is a chronological list of some of the major biblical sites in Israel. It is not exhaustive.

Old Testament Sites

Mount Moriah Abraham was told to offer his son Isaac in the land of Moriah on a mountain that the Lord would show him (Gen. 22:2). Later, David bought the threshing floor of Araunah for 50 shekels of silver and built an altar there (2 Sam. 24:21). Solomon erected the first Temple above that altar. Today, the "Temple Mount" contains the Dome of the Rock, which tourists view from the Mount of Olives.

Beersheba: Abraham and Abimelech made a covenant at Beersheba (Gen. 1:27), and Abraham dug a well there (Gen. 21:30). The servants of Isaac also built a well there (Gen. 28:23-25). Today, there are two wells some distance apart. The larger one is 12½ feet in diameter and 44½ feet deep. The other one is 5 feet in diameter and 42 feet deep. Water is pure and sweet in both of them. These wells are probably not the exact ones that Abraham and Isaac's servants built, but this is the historical site of Beersheba.

Hebron: Abraham buried his wife Sarah in the cave of Machpelah in Hebron (Gen. 23:1-20, esp. 19). Later, Abraham was buried there (Gen. 25:7-10), and so were Isaac (Gen. 35:28-29), Rebecca, Jacob (Gen. 47:28-30; 50:1-14), and Leah (Gen. 49:31).

Herod the Great (31-4 BC) built a large, rectangular enclosure over the cave. The stone walls were 6 feet thick and at least 3 feet tall. and sometimes 24 feet long. It is the only fully surviving Herodian structure from the Hellenistic Judaism period. The Herodian building stands on an earlier structure, possibly built in the 2nd century BC. In 2020, archaeologists dated pottery from the caves to the 8th century BC. The site may have been a pilgrimage site as early as this date.

Jericho The city of Jericho is thought to be one of the oldest cities in the world. Its location has changed very little throughout the ages. It was the first city Joshua conquered as he entered the land.

Hazor Joshua conquered Hazor (Joshua 11:10-11). Solomon built the walls of Jerusalem, Hazor, Megiddo, and Gezer (1 Kings 9:15). The remains at Hazor, Megiddo, and Gezer show a highly distinctive six-chambered gate, as well as a characteristic style in its administration buildings. I attended a lecture by archaeologistWilliam G. Dever, who argued that this archaeological discovery demonstrates that there was a United Kingdom at the time of Solomon.

Gideon's Spring Tourists visit the spring where Gideon's men were tested by the way they drank the water (Judges 7:2-7).

Saul's Palace In 1922-23, William Albright excavated Tell el-Ful (Gibeah), located in northern Jerusalem. It is believed to be Saul's palace/fortress (1 Sam. 11:4), but there is some doubt because of subsequent construction over the site and a lack of extensive archaeological work.

Mount Gilboa Tourists visit the site at the foot of Mount Gilboa, where Saul and his three sons died in battle (1 Sam. 31:1-10).

En Gedi David hid from King Saul in the caves of the En Gedi oasis (1 Sam. 23:29), which is near the Dead Sea. David spared Saul's life in a cave there, cutting only a corner of his robe to prove his loyalty (1 Sam. 24:1-22). While at En Gedi, David wrote Psalms 57 and 142. Tourists visit the waterfall there.

Samaria Ahab built an ivory "house" in Samaria (1 Kings 22:39), a reference to his palace. Archaeologists have discovered a palace complex in Samaria that includes an inner courtyard, storerooms, evidence of a surrounding wall, and over 250 ivory fragments.

Megiddo Joshua conquered Megiddo (Joshua 12:7, 21). Solomon raised a levy to build "the wall of Jerusalem, Hazor, Megiddo, and Gezer (1 Kings 9:15). Archaeologists have discovered a water tunnel Megiddo built in the ninth century BC. It consists of a 100–115-foot vertical shaft and a 200-230-foot horizontal tunnel. It is often associated with King Solomon's fortification effort, but the system itself is typically dated to the later period of Ahab.

Hezekiah's Tunnel Around 700 BC, Hezekiah built a tunnel, known as the Siloam Tunnel, from the Gihon Spring outside the wall of Jerusalem to the Pool of Siloam inside Jerusalem. (2 Kings 20:20; 1 Chron. 32:2-4, 30). The tunnel is 583 yards long, about ⅓ of a mile. In 1884, an inscription just inside the entrance from the pool of Sidon was discovered. According to the inscription, the tunnel was carved out of solid rock, with two teams, one starting at each end of the tunnel, meeting in the middle. Part of the inscription is unreadable. It is in a museum in Istanbul, Turkey. Tourists can walk through the tunnel.

The Temple Mount As noted before, Abraham was told to offer his son Isaac on a mountain in Moriah (Gen. 22:2). Later, David built an altar there (2 Sam. 24:21). Solomon erected the first Temple above that altar. Solomon's Temple was destroyed in 586 BC. It was later rebuilt by Zerubbabel and remodeled by Herod the Great. That Temple was destroyed by the Romans in AD 70.

When Caliph Omar conquered Jerusalem in 638, he found the Temple Mount area strewn with ruins and desolate. Because it was considered to be the site of Mohammed's miraculous night journey and the holiest shrine of Islam after Mecca and Medina, Omar erected a wooden mosque there. In 691, Caliph Abdel-Malik erected the **Dome of the Rock**, a golden crown mosque, looking much as it does now. In 710, the silver-domed **al-Aqsa Mosque** was built on the traditional site of Solomon's Palace and the Palace of the kings of Judah.

Today, tourists view the Temple Mount and the Dome of the Rock from the Mount of Olives. They also visit the Western Wall, known as the **Wailing Wall,** the retaining wall of Herod's Temple. Since Islam occupies the Temple Mount, Jews pray at the Wailing Wall.

Model On the grounds of the Holy Land Hotel is a model of Jerusalem during the Second Temple period.

New Testament Sites

Bethlehem Rachel, Jacob's favorite wife, is said to be buried on the way to Bethlehem (Gen. 35:19). A small dome structure is said to be her tomb. Bethlehem was the home of Naomi and her family. Ruth gleaned in the fields of Bethlehem and met her kinsman, Boaz. Their great-grandson, David, was born here and Samuel "anointed him in the midst of his brethren" (1 Sam. 16:13).

Jesus was born in Bethlehem (Lk. 2:7). Constantine built the Church of the Nativity over the spot where it is said Jesus was born. A hole was cut in the top of the cave so people could look down into the place where it was said Jesus was born. Today, people can visit that spot. The shepherd's field is where the shepherd heard about the birth of Jesus from "the angel of the Lord" (Lk. 2:9).

Mount of Temptation: While in Jericho, looking toward the mountain range to the south, one sees the Mount of Temptation, where the devil offered Jesus "all the kingdoms of the world" (Lk. 4:5). The Monastery of Karantel is built on the site. Tourists do not visit the site; they only view it from Jericho.

Nazareth Jesus was born in Bethlehem, but He grew up in Nazareth (Mt. 2:21-23; Lk. 4:16). At Nazareth, there are numerous sites pertaining to the life of Jesus, including the church of Joseph, supposedly built above his home and workshop, Mary's well, the Roman Catholic Church of the Annunciation, the Greek Orthodox Church of the Annunciation, the Synagogue Church, where Jesus, "as this custom was went ... into the synagogue on the Sabbath day (Lk. 4:16), and the Chapel of Our Ladies Fear, from where Mary is said to have watched Jesus being "led to the brow of the hill on which the city was built that they might throw him down over the cliff" (Lk. 4:28-29). No tour covers all of these sites. Most tours will cover only one or maybe two.

Two churches claim to be the site of the angel's announcement to Mary that she would be the mother of Jesus: The Roman Catholic Church of the Annunciation and the Greek Orthodox Church of the Annunciation. Which claim is correct?

The Roman Catholic Church of the Annunciation is said to have been commissioned by Constantine, whose mother, Helena, helped found churches commemorating events in the life of Jesus, such as the Church of the Nativity (His birthplace) and the Church of the Holy Sepulcher (His crucifixion and burial). Some versions of it were known to have existed around 570.

The Greek Orthodox Church of the Annunciation's claim is based on the apocryphal Protoevangelium of James, which states that this event occurred while Mary was drawing water from a local spring in Nazareth. The Protoevangelium of James says that Mary was miraculously conceived and was a virgin before and after the birth of Christ. In 405, Pope Innocent condemned it. Around 500, it was classified as apocryphal by the Gelasian Decree.

The Roman Catholic Church of the Annunciation is the more likely site.

Cana Jesus turned water into wine (Jn. 2:1-11) at Cana, a town 4 miles north of Nazareth.

Sychar Jacob built a well at Sychar (Jn. 4:5-6) and Jesus talked to a Samaritan woman there (Jn. 4:4-7). Today, at Nablus, a well, said to be Jacob's well, can be seen in a Greek Orthodox Church.

Capernaum When Jesus left Nazareth, He moved to Capernaum (Mt. 4:13), a village on the northern shore of the Sea of Galilee. It was the hometown of Peter, Andrew, James, John, and Matthew. It became the center of Jesus' ministry. Archaeologists have found a 4th-century synagogue built over a 1st-century one, and a 5th-century church built over an earlier house believed to be Peter's. Jesus preached in the synagogue at Capernaum and healed Peter's mother-in-law at Peter's house (Lk. 4:38-39).

Sea of Galilee The Sea of Galilee is approximately 13 miles long from north to south and 7-8 miles wide at its widest point. It is a shallow lake with a maximum depth of 140-200 feet, about 700 feet below sea level. It is the world's lowest freshwater lake.

The Mount of the Beatitudes Between Capernaum and Tabgha, is where Jesus is said to have preached the Sermon on the Mount (Mt. 5-7). The site is a grassy slope northwest of the Sea of Galilee, offering a clear view of the lake. In 1938, the Church of the Beatitude was built near the site of the 4th-century church. It is built in the shape of an octagon, representing the eight Beatitudes.

Tabgha. In 350, the first church was built to commemorate Jesus' feeding 5000 people with five loaves and two fish (Lk. 9:10-17). It was mentioned by Egeria in 380. Around 480, the church was enlarged, and a mosaic floor was added. The Persians destroyed the church in 614. Archaeologists have discovered a 5th-century church built on the foundation of a smaller 4th-century chapel. In 1984, the current Church of the Multiplication was built to the same floor plan as the 5th-century church. Today, the foundations of the original 4th-century church can also be seen under a glass panel to the right of the altar. In front of the altar is the 5th-century mosaic depicting two fish flanking a basket containing five loaves of bread.

Also at Tahha is the Sanctuary of the Primacy, which is where, after the resurrection, Jesus appeared to the disciples, ate with them, and told Peter to feed the sheep (Jn. 21:1-19). The current church was built in 1933 and incorporates part of the earlier 4th-century church.

Caesarea Philippi In the first century, the city of Caesarea Philippi was notorious for its intense idolatry, featuring the Grotto of Pan, temples to Zeus and Augustus, and a court for the goddess Nemesis. It is located in the northern Golan Heights at the foot of Mount Herman, 15 miles north of the Sea of Galilee, 37 miles from Capernaum. The natural spring near Caesarea Philippi is the largest source of water for the Jordan River. It was here that Jesus asked Peter, "Who do men say that I, the Son of Man, am?" (Mt. 16:13).

Bethany Lazarus, Martha, and Mary lived in Bethany, a town on the Mount of Olives, where there is a church named the Sanctuary of St. Lazarus. Jesus raised Lazarus from the dead there (Jn. 11:1-44). The traditional site of Lazarus' tomb is nearby.

The Inn of the Good Samaritan Between Jerusalem and Jericho, is the Inn of the Good Samaritan that commemorates where Jesus told the parable of the good Samaritan (Lk. 10:30-36).

The Mount of Olives The Mount of Olives is a mountain ridge east of Jerusalem's Old City. It is 2.2 miles long and as high as 2710 feet. It is higher than the city of Jerusalem, which is 2474 feet high. The Hebron Valley is between the Mount of Olives and Jerusalem.

Several events in the life of Jesus took place on the Mount of Olives. From there, Jesus wept over Jerusalem (Mt. 23:37-39; Lk. 13:34-35; 19:41-44), healed Lazarus (Jn. 11:1-44), and delivered the Olivet discourse (Mt. 24-25). The Garden of Gethsemane is at the foot of the Mount of Olives. Jesus ascended from the Mount of Olives (Acts 1:9-12).

The Garden of Gethsemane Inside The Church of All Nations, a church sponsored jointly by several countries, is a rock, the Rock of Agony, which is said to be bedrock where Jesus prayed before He was arrested (Mark 14:32 -42).

The House of Caiaphas During His trials, Jesus was taken to the house of Caiaphas, the High Priest. It was there that Peter denied the Lord. At Caiaphas's house, there is a prison thought to be where Jesus spent the rest of the night after He appeared before

Caiaphas. It is not mentioned in the Bible.

The Church of the Holy Sepulcher The original church was built in 325. It contains the traditional site where Jesus was crucified at Calvary or Golgotha, and the traditional site of the tomb where He was buried and resurrected.

Gordon's Calvary In 1882, the British General Gordon was an advocate for the area near the Damascus Gate as the site of the crucifixion. Archaeologist Kathleen Kenyon said the nearby tomb was a first-century tomb (Jn. 19:41). This site is not the crucifixion and burial of Jesus, but it gives tourists an idea of what the tomb of Jesus looked like.

The Ascension of Jesus: The Chapel of the Ascension on the Mount of Olives is the traditional site of Jesus' ascension to heaven. A small stone slab in the center of the shrine features a natural indentation believed to be the right footprint of Jesus Christ, marking His final point of contact with the earth before ascending to heaven.

Joppa Jonah departed from Joppa to go to Tarsus (Jonah 1:3). Joppa was the home of Tabitha, whom Peter raised from the dead (Acts 9:36–42). At Joppa, Peter spent time in the home of Simon the tanner (Acts 9:43) and, on Simon's rooftop, he saw the vision of unclean animals (Acts 10:9-16). At Joppa, tourists can see what is said to be the home of Simon the tanner.

Caesarea On the Mediterranean coast sits the city of Caesarea. It was significantly enlarged by Herod the Great, who dedicated the town and its port to Caesar Augustus as Caesarea. Herod built his palace on a promontory jutting out into the sea, with a decorative pool. The Roman aqueduct brought water from the foot of the Carmel range to Caesarea. In 6 BC, Caesarea replaced Jerusalem as the capital and became the official residence of its governors, such as Pontius Pilatus. In 1961, a slab was found at Caesarea bearing an inscription in Latin naming Tiberius, Pilatus, and Judaea.

Philip lived in Caesarea (Acts 8:40). The centurion, Cornelius, lived in Caesarea and was baptized there by Peter (Acts 10:1-48). Paul spent time in Philip's house in Caesarea (Acts 21:8). Paul was a prisoner in Caesarea for two years before being sent to Rome (Acts 23:23; 25:1-13).

The Dead Sea The Dead Sea, which is the lowest point on the face of the earth at 1290 feet, is shrinking. In 1985, it was 48 miles long and 11 miles across. In 2026, it was 31 miles long and 9 miles wide. It is more than 10 times saltier than ocean water.

Qumran The Qumran community is located 6 miles south of Jericho, about a mile from the northwest shore of the Dead Sea. It was inhabited by the Essenes, a highly ritualistic Jewish sect. The Dead Sea Scrolls were found nearby.

Masada: Herod the Great rebuilt Masada, which sits atop a 20-acre plateau, as a pleasure palace, including hanging gardens, a swimming pool, an elaborate bathhouse, various stores, a synagogue, and ritual baths. When the Romans attacked Jerusalem in AD 70, 960 Jewish zealots, men, women, and children barricaded themselves on Masada and held it for three years. In AD 73, when the Romans built a ramp to attack, the zealots committed suicide. Each man killed his family and 10 men were chosen by lot to slay the rest. Then, they cast lots for themselves. A few survived to tell the story (Josephus, *War of the Jews*, VII: 9:1). Tourists visit the site via cable car.

Chapter 7

The Spiritual Benefit

Tours of Israel focus on history, geography, and biblical events. That is beneficial, but does not necessarily include the spiritual benefit. Beyond the knowledge of history and geography, what is the spiritual benefit of the tour of Israel?

The Spiritual Benefit

God revealed spiritual truth at different times and places. Paul says that the things that happened to Israel "happened to them as examples, and they were written for our admonition" (1 Cor. 10:11). So, at each place in Israel where a biblical event happened, the question that needs to be asked is, "What spiritual truth was taught here?"

A Suggestion

It is unrealistic to probe every spiritual truth for every event that happened at every place where the tours stop. But at least at some of the most significant stops, the spiritual truth revealed there needs to be considered.

Read the Relevant Passages At some stops, at least read the pertinent passages. For example, when David was hiding from Saul at En Gedi, he wrote Psalms 57 and 142. Why not at least read them standing at the waterfall at En Gedi?

Explain the Relevant Passages At some places, the pertinent passage should be briefly explained. At Caesarea Philippi, after the guide explained in detail the pagan nature of the situation in the first century, I briefly explained Matthew 16:13-17 in about 10 minutes. In a pagan environment, the question is, "Who is Jesus Christ?" He is the Christ, meaning the Messiah, the Son of God.

One of the places where this should definitely be done is where Jesus preached the Sermon on the Mount. Again, in about 10 minutes, I explained that the subject of the Sermon on the Mount is real righteousness (Mt. 5:20). Then, I outlined the sermon as follows.

Introduction (Mt. 5:1-20)
I. Real righteousness has the right precepts 5:21-48
    1. Murder and anger 5:21-26 (love others).
    2. Adultery and lust 5:27-30.
    3. Divorce and remarriage 5:31-32.
    4. Oaths and speech 5:33-37.
    5. Retaliation and love 5:38-42 (love others).
    6. Neighbors and Enemies 5:43-48 (love your enemies).

II. Real righteousness has the right practices 6:1-18.
   1. Giving 6:1-4 (as unto the Lord).
   2. Praying 6:5-15 (as unto the Lord).
   3. Fasting 6:16-18 (as unto the Lord).
III. Real righteousness has the right principles 6:19-7:11
   1. Do not lay up treasure on earth 6:19-24 (serve God, 6:24).
   2. Do not be anxious 6:25-34 (trust God, 6:30)
   3. Do not Judge 7:1-6 (minister to others).
   4. Pray 7:7-11 (depend on the Lord).
Conclusion: Love fulfills the Law 7:12
   1. Enter 7:13-14.
   2. Beware 7:15-23.
   3. Hear and do 7:24-27.

The subject of the Sermon on the Mount is real righteousness and a large part of that is living a loving life. The sermon also places great emphasis on rewards. Thus, the point of the Sermon on the Mount is that those living a righteous and loving life will be rewarded in the kingdom.

Another great opportunity for explaining a passage is in the upper room. Once more, in about 10 minutes, I explained that when Jesus washed the disciples' feet, He was teaching them that the loving thing to do is to serve one another.

Other places on the tour offer opportunities to either read or explain passages of Scripture. Doing this adds a spiritual dimension to the tour.

A Simple Guide To Biblical Israel

About The Author

G. Michael Cocoris is a gifted communicator. He can make even complicated subjects simple, clear, and practical. His breadth of experience has allowed him to relate to a wide range of audiences.

Michael received a Bachelor of Arts degree from Tennessee Temple University, a Master of Theology degree from Dallas Seminary, and a Doctorate of Divinity from Biola University. He traveled the United States for over a dozen years as a speaker. He has also been a seminary professor, visiting lecturer, and world traveler, including hosting tours to Israel and China.

Michael has pastored three churches, including a rural church when he was in seminary, an urban church, the historic Church of the Open Door, first in downtown Los Angeles and later in Glendora, California, and a suburban church, the Lindley Church in Tarzana California, a suburb of Los Angeles. While at the Church of Open Door, he had a daily radio broadcast.

Michael has written numerous magazine articles, mainly for *Biblical Research Monthly*. He has authored a number of books, including *Seventy Years on Hope Street, A History of the Church of the Open Door*; *How To Live A Biblical Spiritual Life, Clarifying the Confusion; Repentance, The Most Misunderstood Word in the Bible; Evangelism: A Biblical Approach; The Salvation Controversy; Lordship Salvation: Is It Biblical?; The Books of the Bible, the Subject, Structure, Situation, and Significant Verses of Each Book; Psalms, A Song for Every Situation, Each Summarized on One Page;* and *Counseling Theories, A Biblical Evaluation.* In addition, he was a contributor to The *NKJV Study Bible* and *Nelson's New Illustrated Bible Commentary*.

Michael is the pastor of the Lindley Church in Tarzana, California. He and his wife, Patricia, live in Santa Monica, California.

www.ingramcontent.com/pod-product-compliance
Lightning Source LLC
Chambersburg PA
CBHW050047080526
44586CB00014B/1502